Journey
to the
Moon

Acknowledgments
Executive Editor: Diane Sharpe
Supervising Editor: Stephanie Muller
Design Manager: Sharon Golden
Page Design: Ian Winton
Photography: Science Photo Library: cover (bottom right), pages 11, 13, 15, 17, 19, 25, 29 (both); Tony Stone: cover (middle right).

ISBN 0-8114-3713-2

Copyright © 1995 Steck-Vaughn Company.

1 2 3 4 5 6 7 8 9 00 PO 00 99 98 97 96 95 94

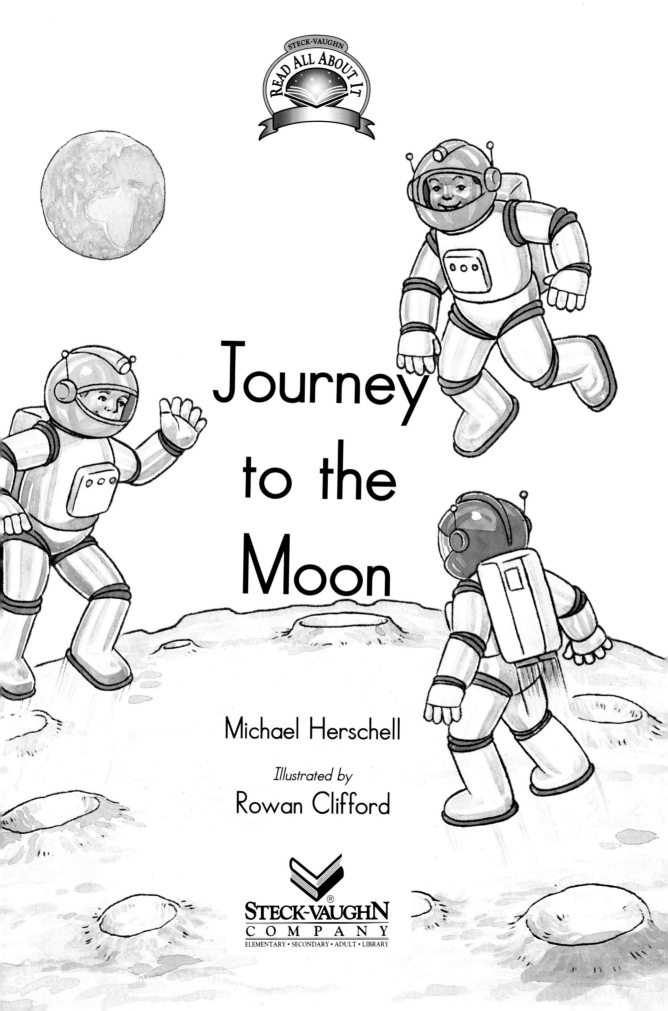

Journey
to the
Moon

Michael Herschell

Illustrated by
Rowan Clifford

STECK-VAUGHN
COMPANY
ELEMENTARY • SECONDARY • ADULT • LIBRARY

The moon is our nearest neighbor in space. But it is still about 240,000 miles away.

I wish we could visit the moon.

We can pretend to visit the moon. Climb into the magic spaceship, and let's go!

6

Earth is one of nine planets that
go around the sun.

Together the planets and the
sun make up what we call the
Solar System.

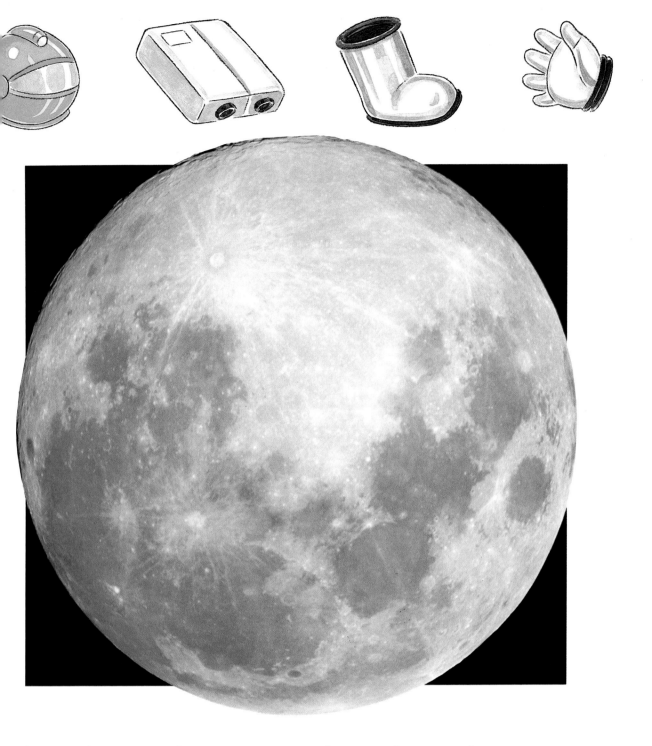

No living things are found on the
moon because there is no air
and no water.

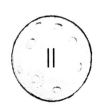
11

The moon does not pull you to the ground as much as the earth does. That is why you can jump so high.

The red planet is Mars. It is
a dry, rocky planet. It is also
very cold.

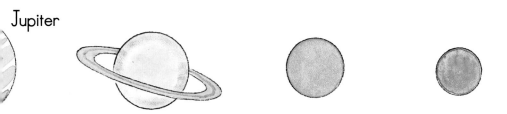

That is Jupiter with its giant red spot. Jupiter is the biggest planet in the Solar System.

The rings around Saturn are
made of pieces of ice and dust.

There is little Pluto!

Pluto is about the size of our moon. It is farther from the sun than any other planet.

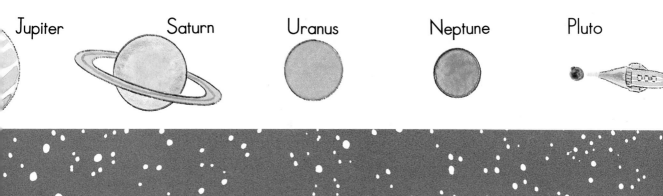

The stars are so far away.
We must travel very fast to get
to the nearest one. Hold on!

23

Groups of stars are called
galaxies. There are thousands
of galaxies. Our galaxy is called
the Milky Way.

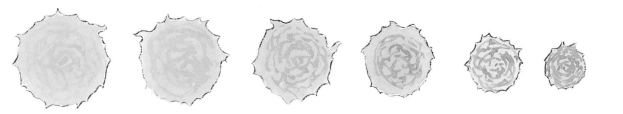

No, stars are all different sizes. The large stars are called supergiants. The small stars are called dwarfs.

Our sun is a small star.

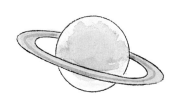

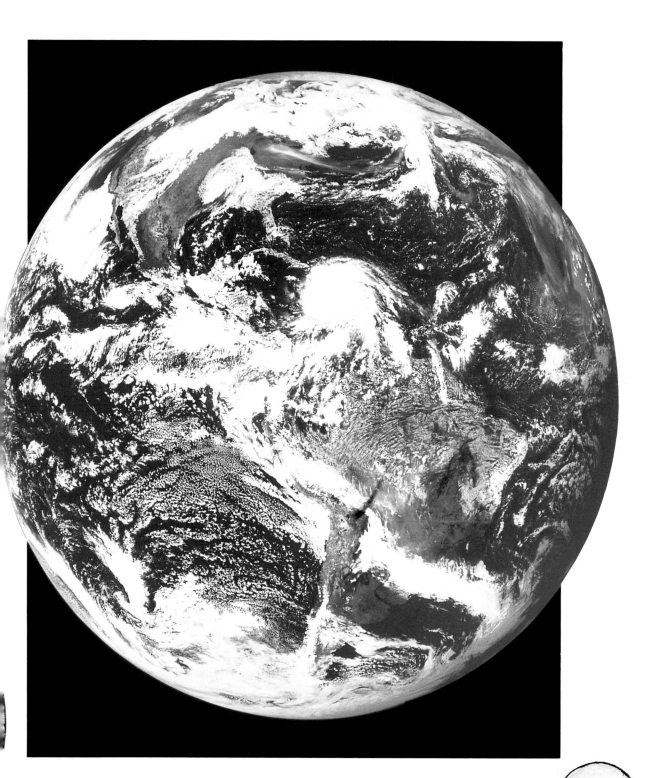

Can you remember the names
of the nine planets?

30

Index

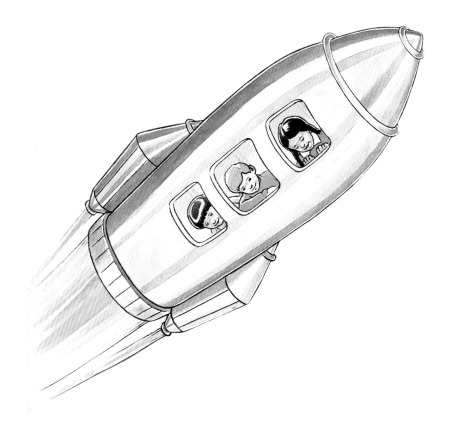